# qarrtsiluni
online literary magazine

*Qarrtsiluni is an experiment in online literary and artistic collaboration. The title comes from an Iñupiaq word that means "sitting together in the darkness, waiting for something to burst."*

*The online journal began publishing on September 20, 2005; our first print issue was the September-December issue, 2008.*

*We encourage you to visit our website, where in addition to all the material presented here, you will find audio files of the authors reading their own work, music and video contributions to the theme, full-color reproductions of all the images, comments from readers, and responses from the authors.*

www.qarrtsiluni.com

*Beth Adams and Dave Bonta*

managing editors

*Brittany Larkin*

editorial assistant

ISBN 978-0-9781749-7-2

PHOENICIA PUBLISHING
MONTREAL

# economy

june - august 2009

The word Economy has its roots in Greek - *oikos* and *nomos* - meaning the principles necessary to maintain the household. It's a thoughtful word. The study of economics, until the 18th century, was a branch of philosophy. And in 2009, as the global economy struggled to find its way to recovery, we decided to take this much-used word and ask artists to play around with its meaning and implication so that it might be re-envisioned.

Contributors were challenged to send us interpretive and imaginative explorations of this one word - and our challenge, as editors, was to select from the rowdy, triumphant, and eclectic mix of poems, flash fiction, visual artwork, and video poetry that resulted.

We then had the difficult and stimulating task of choosing work we believe depicted the word beyond its stereotypical associations. We sought out submissions that weren't so much about the news of the word but about its heart and heat. It was a real honor to read through, select and then present the brave and beautiful work in the Economy issue of qarrtsiluni, which engaged its audience to read and think in new and wonderful ways.

And it goes without saying that we are delighted to learn that Beth and Dave, as qarrtsiluni's managing editors, consider the issue worthy of being added to their wonderful stable of print editions.

*Anna Dickie and Pamela Hart*
editors

**economy of line** by Michael Aanji Crowley, pg. 28

# Contents

# Tilting

*Anna Dickie; photos by Robert Mellin*

Tilting is a remote village on Fogo Island, eight miles off the Newfoundland shore. I discovered its existence recently after hearing extracts from Robert Mellin's study of the place as part of an edition of *Something Understood,* produced by Falling Tree Productions for BBC Radio 4.

Mellin, an architect and professor of architecture at McGill University in Montreal, purchased a house in Tilting after falling in love with the area. That led to his extraordinary work recording the vernacular architecture of the village, and indeed the area, and capturing the voice and spirit of a fast-disappearing way of life. Tilting, one of 11 communities on the island, has seen its population decline from about 500 hundred residents to about 300 in the past few years.

In his study, Mellin trains his architect's eye on wooden houses, sheds, fishing platforms, fences, root stores, and tools. His quest for knowledge of the particular depicts the essence of a remote community that lives and works with the grain of the land, the sea, and the weather. Mellin's book, *Tilting: House Launching, Slide Hauling, Potato Trenching, and Other Tales from a Newfoundland Fishing Village,* was published by Princeton Architectural Press in New York, and won the Winterset Literary Award in 2003.

In preparing for this edition of qarrtsiluni it seemed appropriate to feature something on Tilting. Thanks to the wonderful economy of communication that is the Internet, I was able to contact Robert Mellin, who has kindly allowed us to include four photographs of Tilting. He also helped us secure the necessary permissions from Falling Tree Productions and Rick Boland, who reads the piece, to present an audio clip titled, "Ted Burke on Hospitality."

1. Cyril McGrath taking his sheep to Pigeon Island in Tilting
2. Restored Albert Dwyer Premises, Tilting, Fogo Island, Newfoundland
3. Gladys McGrath with two of her grandchildren in her kitchen in Tilting

# The New Poetry

*Ray Templeton*

He wrote his verse in smileys:
expressive punctuation, soul laid bare
in variations on the colon and parenthesis,

a kiss to make up with an asterisk,
collusion in a semi-colon wink,
sleep with one stroke, sickness with another,

death dealt with his two fingers —
the keyboard skull and crossbones,
using eight and X.

He excelled at concrete imagery:
roses made from ats and brackets,
percentages for clover.

He made the most of metaphors
on cows and monkeys,
pigs and chickens.

That year he swept the board
at all the major competitions
despite complaints from purists,

and the old guard raging
that symbols couldn't rhyme.
But others got the point:

anything to lift the art
from dusty books and droning readings
can't be bad. His limelight period

didn't last, though: there were queries
about his methods, he made a hash
of his defence. Quotes

in the papers spoke of scandal —
he lost the next year's smiley slam,
and his career just …

# Sojourn

*Gerard Wozek*

Saint Alphonsus instructed his followers:
"Take only what you need." Retreating into
the desert, he lived for three weeks eating
volcanic ash, waiting on Uriel's command.
After twenty days he was flame, his mind,
the arc of sky. He no longer felt his toes
scraping hot sands. He walked unharmed
past rattlesnakes, blended into copper hillsides,
drank from arid sage plants. The ascetic turned
into wind, moving effortlessly over mountains,
branches of tall cypress. Years later, clerics
found his rotted sandals, placed them as a relic
amid hair and purported bones of local saints.
Believers still come to place their hands
on the worn insteps where Alphonsus stood
looking into the archangel's eyes. Supplicants
touch desert dust to tongues, reverently bow,
attempt to cast off everything but their marrow.

# Patty Cake

*Karen Stromberg*

The moment she knew she'd conceived she made two decisions: no doctors, no birth.

"Baby," she said to the cluster of 15 cells adhering to her uterine wall. "Forgive me. It's a harsh world. I can only think of one way out."

Every cell of their collective body agreed. At the end of nine months there were no contractions, no birth.

By the end of the first in-utero year he slept through the night and drummed on her lower left rib if he wanted a shot of caffeine. He liked reruns of Myron Floren on the Lawrence Welk Show and did not care for Chinese food.

She filled with song. He learned to crack his thumbs in time to her voice, a double-jointedness which ran through the family on her father's side.

By the third year she began to thin. Lying nude in the backyard dosing them both with Vitamin D, she noticed how translucent her flesh had become, the centerline full of white striations pulling and stretching like a seam coming undone.

In the dome of her belly, two small hands pressed, and then between them, a face. Even pale and waterlogged, his hair a floating nimbus, he looked exactly like her uncle Vinnie. She smiled. The boy smiled back.

His finger with its long curled nail followed the path of a crow over the dome of his world, leaving a flush of pink in the fluid.

She called her sister, said she was leaving a present in the backyard. The sister said she'd be right over.

When the sister arrived, the boy, sitting upright in the pelvic girdle, was playing patty-cake in a small puddle of amniotic fluid, tears streaming down his face from the pure brilliance of the day.

# The New Economy

*Rob A. Mackenzie*

The rattling cans fell silent and the rattlers
stiffened to attention, equidistant,
as if on military display.

On the clearing's far side, a massive hangar,
slabbed together with corrugated iron,
stewed in the sun's gut.

One door, no windows. "You live there?"
Laughter churned through the ranks.
One woman spoke,

"This building is the last hope for Speckland,
a hut of refuge for its people,
a slim dignity.

Here, those forced into tiny squats in Leith,
twelve to a room, with only Speckish
supermarkets

for nutrition, can now find fulfilment
and five-minute toilet breaks
while studying

the language of Shakespeare and Thatcher
by selling off last year's mobile
phone technology."

At that moment, the door opened and a shock
of ragged men, women and children
tumbled out,

sharing cigarettes, pulling open Kraft lunch boxes
and cans of Coke Zero, setting
alarms to vibrate.

"For six pounds a month, you can feed
a child a week of recycled meat.
For twelve,

a family can be trucked out from the city.
For five hundred, your name
will be immortalised

in Speck City on a plaque of solid aluminium.
Please give generously, we rely
on your gifts."

# The Steel

*Steve Rago*

Entrance, Bethlehem Steel Plant

These black-and-white pinhole photographs show how the iconic Bethlehem (Pennsylvania) steel plant—"The Steel" to those who worked there—appeared in 2005. The sprawling complex sat dark, rusting, and abandoned behind chain link fencing.

The plant, which closed in 1998, had fueled the economic engines of the 20th Century, providing the ribs for battleships, skyscrapers, bridges, and the interstate highway system. This year, part of the historic site has been developed into a Sands Casino and Resort.

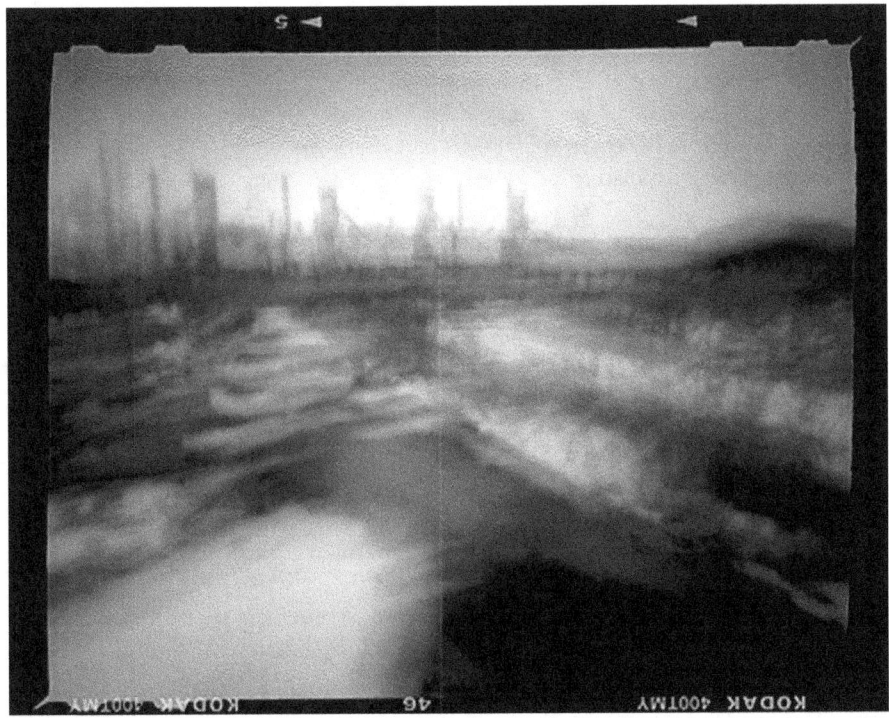

Empty Lot and Towers, Bethlehem Plant

While some of the lesser buildings have been bulldozed, the blast furnaces and several other core components remain. The Sands has said the tall furnaces will be repainted and illuminated with "architectural lighting."

# From *Earth Records*

*Alistair Noon*

You sign your name, and live, as long-term guest,
the economics of the domicile:
the highest prices start where views are best.
Light has status. One pays for space and style.
Descending from these peaks, the roofs begin
to terrace out across each marked-off plot.
The postcode scores the loss or draw or win.
Sometimes the height is shared, and sometimes not.
You'll find the horizontal villa, or
the block of income worry, standing tall.
A bench in central London costs no more
than dangerous nights, a policeman's wake-up call.
In any case, the place that's always free
is where the land breathes out, becoming sea.


\*


A different kind of music sprays the pavements
in the summers of economic booms:
trained violinists play for unit payments;
grandmothers, graduates amortize rooms.
The raising of the GDP includes
sales of Sleeping Beauty by teenage boys
in stations; seminars that teach the moods
suited to business, the interview ploys.
Private coaches are the sleeker design,
the comfier; brighter the books and shops.
The local film moves quickly into line—
the new heroes: brick-faced boxers and cops.
The higher prices crush the ticket crush,
and chums count less. The new pavements are flush.

## Our Rowdy Pack Song  a hay(na)ku*

*Holly Anderson and Caroline Beasley-Baker*

dented
moon, wheeling
just like me.

synaptic trash
caught sweet
in blue-violet mercies

roaring,
glory-headed girl,
smashed diamond skies

tilt,
tilt a-whirl,
twist and all-fall-down.

dry
river coursing
bloodstream's ancient dreams

sashay
into beatitude
unravelling like me,

glistering
somersault into
infinity's unformed matter

—is
that fire-
eating the open door?

or
peat-y fingers
down my throat?

i'm-a-ring-'round-rosie-girl,
a hot-blue-star
unhitched and free-wheeling

one-of-seven-sisters,
a pleiade,
bartering my soul.

unbolt
this cage
of inkblue heaven

drown
my mercies,
fill my mouth,

cast-me
deep beyond
the oh-so-watchful stars,

deepsky,
non-stellar objects
wheeling lopsided within.

*Hay(na)ku is a 21st century verse form invented by poet and publisher Eileen R. Tabios, who launched the first Hay(na)ku challenge to the world at large via the web on June 12, 2003 (Philippine Independence Day). The "traditional" form of a hay(na)ku entails:*

    *\* A tercet: 3 lines.*
    *\* A total of 6 words: 1 in the first line, 2 in the second line, and 3 in the third line.*
    *\* There is no restriction on syllables, stresses, or rhymes.*

*Then, in 2007, Tabios issued an online invitation to poets to join in groups of three or more to create "chain" hay(na)ku with each tercet moving between voices as in a conversation or a tra-ditional "parts" song. "Our Rowdy Pack Song" is a poetic duet that loosely interprets the form.*

# The Supper at Emmaus

*Irene Brown*

*The Supper at Emmaus*
just over,
Caravaggio's Christ
stood in the Tube
dressed in jeans
and shapeless jumper
holding a jacket
for his girl.

*Note: I wrote this poem in 2005 after having been to the exhibition* Caravaggio: The Final Years *at the National Gallery in London which included his painting* The Supper at Emmaus. *This year, I came across and read the Salley Vickers novel,* The Other Side of You, *which featured the painting in its theme. I saw it again drawn in chalk on a Florence pavement by a Texan artist, Kelly Borsheim, and her students.*

# What the Forest Said

*Jessamyn Smyth*

Tell me.

      Which part?

All of it. Any of it. Just—something vivid.

    -

      I was walking.

Yes?

      And there were two deer.

Whitetails?

      Yes, whitetails, flashing alarm. They heard the dog. I didn't tell him; he was looking for a good stick, something nice to throw. The deer flipped their tails and danced away. I could see reflections of yellow beech leaves in the eye of one of them, turned toward me: she was that close.

    -

Tell me another.

      I don't know what to tell you.

Please.

    -

      Bobwhites.

What?

      Six or seven of them, exploding from the underbrush with wing-beats so loud I ducked. The dog ran so fast he ran right out of the orange t-shirt I put on him to differentiate him from bear.

Bear?

      It's bear season. They're shooting bears.

---

Oh.

He treed them.

The bears?

The bobwhites. They were furious.

I bet he was proud.

Very proud.

-

You're going to leave, aren't you.

Yes.

Soon?

Probably. There isn't much left.

There is. There could be—

Shhhhh.

-

One more. Tell me one more.

-

Once I walked into the woods and there was only one way: further in. I walked
and walked, and I was fierce and beautiful and brave and resourceful and I
had many adventures, but I was getting tired. Very tired. I couldn't walk any
more, finally; I couldn't be fierce and beautiful and resourceful and brave any
more. Also? I was bored with myself. With all of it. I dug a fire-pit, lined it with
stones. I gathered wood, and made a fire. I was so hungry, but I had nothing to
eat and I was too tired to do anything else, so I sat by the fire and watched the
flames. I figured I'd probably die of starvation eventually, but really, the flames
felt good and I couldn't think what else to do. A stag came out of the forest,
walked right up to the edge of the fire across from me. We looked at each other
for a long time, and I thought: how beautiful. After a while, he lay down across
the fire and split himself open, his blood steaming in the coals. I ate his flesh,
and was restored.

That didn't happen.

No?

No.

-

-

I saw a peregrine eat a bat today.

Yeah?

-

-

You're going, aren't you.

I'm going.

-

I have an idea.

Yeah?

When I go, just look away.

-

Okay.

-

-

Now? Should I look away now?

## February Day Trip

*Susan Donnelly*

That we didn't, after all,
go anywhere that day
hardly matters, looking back.

We discussed it in each other's arms,
weathervaned the state,
considered lakes, obscure museums,

unknown and nearby towns,
and mind-explored some routes
to be later found, or not,

on the toast-distracted map
unfolded over what
was fast becoming lunch.

Next there were the tasks
we ought to do before
we started out:

the laundry,
e-mail,
something we'd forgot.

All the while the sun,
which always plans ahead,
rolled on its grudging round,

Time's chariot.
And yet,
we traveled, looking back.

# underneath is snow

*Stacy Elaine Dacheux*

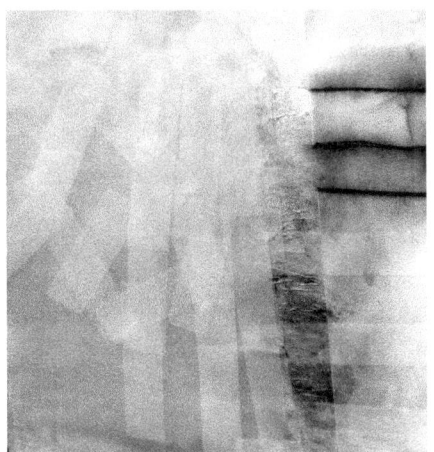

"we were thinking of our bodies as snowsuits instead, thinking this would make us pretty."

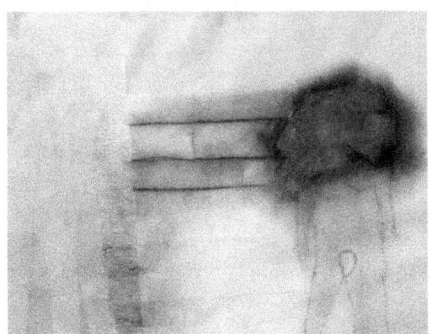

## No Diminishing Returns

*Tom Sheehan*

We talk fifty miles over wire, a mile
for each year since our eyes touched.
Legends still vibrate in your voice, fables,
story of a stray star, Atlantis provoked,
burst meadow beyond the hill, bedding down,
a tree counting the darkness, flower in a field
of rye. I remember a winter clean as salt,
memorialized snow banks, foreign country

of a couch thickly green and awkward
as landed amphibian, a blue wool skirt
of accordion pleats I blew smoke into,
my ear on its blue sky listening to stars
inside, eyes closed, mouth opened,
stretching, reaching, turning corners.

# Need

*Gregory Stapp*

Tell me this poem doesn't exist on paper and needs
the red movement of a mouth.
Tell me you are in the poem.
Your lips wrap every word,
brown packaging, mailed first-class,
for the trip across the country between us.
Tell me we'll never say this poem.
Tell me we can ride through
today in a winter of quiet.

The only papers in my wallet are lists—
groceries and wishes. Tell me these things
fill the blank flat space in its folds.
Don't speak of emptiness or silence.

Emptiness hitched across the country,
silence filled the country.

# Economy of the Untamable

*Jane Rice*

1

I know the road
hangs by a thread

swiftly moss, sudden trees

pieces of sound
come like fish when called

say rain, say spiral
eyes murmur
so it is

breath can't be simple, can it
everydayness of afternoon

breath can't find
can't be simple, can it

roots on a slant
get used to loneliness

salt, hemispheres, glass
break into sky

taste extends
as avalanche
quiet network of hieroglyphs

2

Night seasons
I speak a streaming wind

thrash, throw myself at corners
far off, hidden, lurking

under this lid of cloth, this flap of lawn

how hard to say
only what's inside

every step sinks
myriad bees

widen my mouth
do you hear me

awake at the bottom of the glass

3

Why do I
speak hard things

days consume
let the sea

why do I
almost dwell in silence
speak hard things

alone—eyes
easy isn't simple

without the sea
noise melts into hills

4

Any minute
is there then a world
night speck
what distracts me
is there then
a world
are these grains or dust
a world
how far can I fling
myself from sleep
how far
any minute
myself from sleep
effort coils
without face

without road
neither grain nor dust
any minute
a world

5

Underwater thickens sky

let me lie here
alphabetize myself

whatever you do, please, don't come and go
whatever you do, please

thoughts ridge
unending

what if part of me all of me
into matchbooks

underwater thickens
part of me all of me

can't stay like this

here the absence
here the drums

# Let Go

*Christopher Woods*

The goal now, as you see it, is to get home. The front has come in early. Wind jars the car on the asphalt. The rain comes hard and cold, makes flashlight beams of streetlights. It's hard to drive, but it's also hard to steer. Maybe one too many boilermakers with buddies at Nightlite. But who can blame you, even if you had been good about staying on the wagon for three months, since Liza left.

She hasn't sent as much as a postcard. You watch her credit card charges on your bill, then throw it away. You tell yourself you won't check the mail again until it's time for the unemployment checks to come. Four years in the sausage room at Don's Deluxe Meats didn't mean a thing in the end. No gratitude, no severance pay. Let go without any ceremony at all.

If you can just get home, you'll be okay. The streets are filling with water. You imagine you are the captain of a boat in strong currents. But you do find a way to stop at Discount Package Store for two fifths of cheap bourbon. That will get you through tonight, and maybe more.

At last you reach your street, hit the curb twice, coming to a stop in front of your dark house. You stagger up the walk, and you can hear them bark. They watch you through the window. The welcome wagon. They have waited, the faithful boys, Lewis and Clark.

You feed them and let them run outside in the rain. They come in, shake off the wet night, and lie down at your feet. You gulp the bourbon and watch them. First one, then the other, falls asleep. Let go. Begin dog dreams.

You think that dreaming is best in a warm, dry room. Better still if outside the darkness howls. What do they dream about? Old hunts, saliva, instinct. In a lurching pack under a grey dawn sky, waiting for a waterfowl kill.

Or do they dream of being human, inside a warm house on a wild night. Sitting back, plastered, watching the dogs dream.

## Dealing With Family and Friends

*Karyn Eisler and Dorothee Lang*

When she thought of economy, she thought of social exchange theory—the idea that relationships are based on give and take; our feelings about relationships rest on perceptions of the balance between what we get out of them and what we put in. Usually, she wouldn't have put her thoughts on paper, but this time she did—as concisely as possible, using the medium of the postcard which embodies economy of words (few) and form (small).

The small print, barely legible, made her think of the papers she'd signed that morning—typical legalistic transaction papers that detailed who gave how much for what: 23 Euro for temporary ownership of a compact car, fully insured.

Now for a tobacco shop, to get some stamps. Driving down the bay road, she scanned for the yellow sign, partly wishing she wouldn't find one. Yet, there it was. Exactly four minutes later it was done—the stamp bought, glued to the card, the card on the way, like her again, and her thoughts. Small print, she concluded, is invisible with family and friends, even though it's always part of the subtext; unstated and implicit yet ever-present, like a PS suggesting an afterthought of little importance—which, in social exchange, really isn't.

## Gift Section

*Irene Brown*

| | |
|---|---|
| Got In laws? | Frozen Thoughts? |
| Get Indigestion | Finding Trinkets? |
| Give Indiscriminately | Festive Trap? |
| God! Incense | Frank's Turn |
| Give Imaginatively? | Forget That! |
| Grab It | From This |
| Get I It | For Tuppence |

3 for2

That'll Do!

# Penny

*Rachel Dacus*

A pip, a tip, once a minute
of parking, its worth snipped,
a coin less in diameter or value
than a nickel yet brighter, warm sun
to a five-cent moon—so how did it roll
down to ground level, flat
disc lying unretrieved on streets,
forlorn beside the parking meters
it can no longer feed?

I'm penny-wise and foolish
about artifacts, keep penny bowls
on bookshelves, as if the penny and I, now middle-
aged, had grown up in the same town,
walked the same streets, rolled to the beach
on Saturdays. The cent has diminished
though not dimmed, while I've dimmed
and enlarged my diameter.
It's natural between old friends, the change
of places. We might be change
made from the same register,
sad breakdowns of a haughty dime
taxed to the minutest, rendered
and reckoned as beyond Caesar's interest, left
to the heart's differently hued
apportion and shine.

# Summer's Orders

*Elizabeth Kate Switaj*

swimming hole or should I say
concrete hexahedron of chlorine
water & washed-off sunblock
                                   was never carefree

someone didn't have a lunch
& deep-end pennies weren't enough
                            for candy bars from QFC

girls layered shredding suits
swam a few laps & announced
            you could lose more weight that way

fatter girls stayed wrapped in towels
until they plunged in hiding blue

& when diving board contests of daring
went too far, lifeguards stopped telling
us to walk & strapped the wounded to backboards
for transport we didn't know
                        their parents couldn't afford

## Problems with Value

*Rachel Fox*

I am not worthy

I breathe in
Approximately one eighth
Of the required amount
Of air to fill my lungs
I tell myself
Make do with that
You greedy
Useless
Stupid
Wasteful
Creature
Spread it thinly
It'll last

I breathe out
Tense
Scared
And hurt

I am
Perhaps
A little hard on myself

# economy of line

*Michael Aanji Crowley*

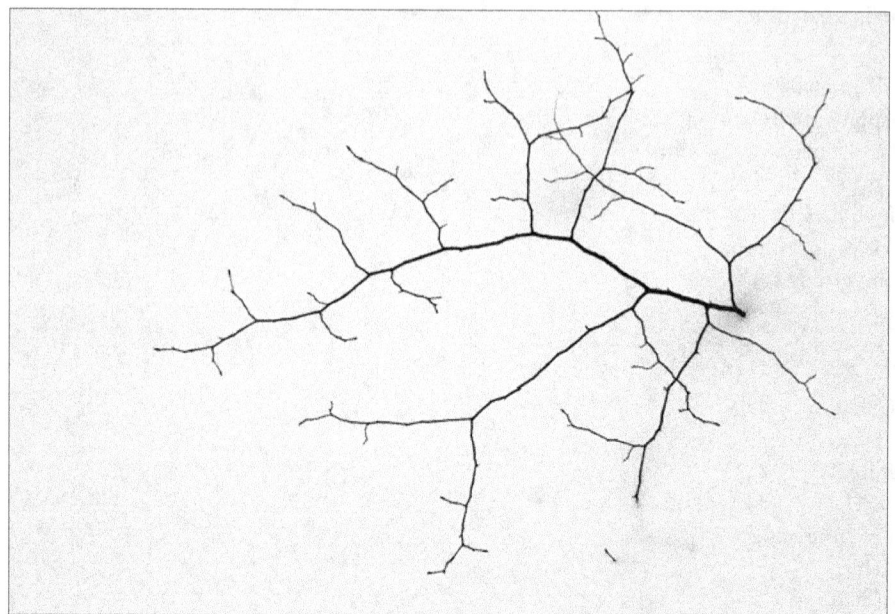

# Binary

*Anne Connolly*

In her devices
a straight line
and a yawning sphere
dance out and in
ad infinitum.
This simple coupling
of one with nothing
fills our void
generates a surge
of order and profusion
as vital as the bang
that brought us here.
Through the bipolar
gateways nano-born
computers stride,
bring see, hear,
taste, touch, smell
to new fruition.
Simple logic.
Only two ways
about it.

# Pushing 1s and 0s

*Holly Wehmeyer*

'Pushing paper' fades
into etymology;
now we push 1s and 0s
from laptops to networks
to internet portals, and
strangers decode our symbols
like Egyptian scribes, creating
stock quotes and photos of hurricanes
and marketing plans for the latest
cell phone.

A security guard glides
through the marble lobby
of a class A office building
in the financial district,
shouting encouragement
to Friday commuters:
"Great job this week,"
he smiles, as if
our tightly packed boulders
of 1s and 0s
would not be waiting for us
at the bottom
of that Monday morning hill.

# What Did the News Say About a Vacation?

*Julene Tripp Weaver*

Something blocks my brain: rain
stuck dewdrops: glisten: listen
impossible to hear: time of
inflated deprivation: waves of
credit: soft porn and fetid kisses:
ears clogged: wet floods force family
evictions: no one hears above
the rift: Daily News: ways to save
pennies: homation: linoleum installation:
stayacation: media invention: report:
birds sing on your deck: remodel,
for a home-vacation: television
trepidation

## Bank Holiday

*Rob A. Mackenzie*

Easter has been cancelled,
now a bank holiday weekend.

There's enough bad news.
No need to nail down the living.

No need to taunt the dead
with resurrection.

Underwood is no banker
but he takes time out

from everyday collapse.
He forks corn from a can.

The mob's rage, he believes,
raised the crucified

three days later,
the resurrection required

a hammering fury.
The banks follow suit,

market exclusive threats
to likely customers,

who queue round the clock
for negative equity.

The banks' hate mail
becomes a status symbol.

People offer their mouths
as personalised ATMs.

Underwood kicks a lamppost.
The mob has been cancelled.

His foot hurts.
Still, he must resist.

# The Huancabamba Depression

*Judith Terzi*

Here in Peru, the Andes change direction
      job markets transmute at home
rain-shadowed landscapes form
      ubiquitous suspension
in dry forests where the cordillera fragments
      as pleasures cloud
deciduous acacia rise in river valleys
      nest eggs drain
sedges and scrophs spread at our feet
      foreclosures germinate
the río Marañón rushes through narrow gorges
      stress tests pressure banks
angel's trumpet boast toxic flowers
      while bonuses startle
the spatuletail and the tapir live endangered
      homelessness surges
here in this tectonic barrier
      depression of credit
outside the level ranges of mountain
      and mood

# Of View

*Anne Morrison Smyth*

# chicken little considers the sky again

*Ed Higgins*

oh, sure i'm still running around like a heads-up/off/prophet/profit/fit trying to cut off my very own de/(con)instruction and all other sordid a•void•able & available/a-Babel towers of post &toastmodern doom/daze re(altho)guarding our economy in/ex/&/anterior terror of too sometimes•always all afright with me henish-looking like some diminutive Kali only i'm in a bantam suit looking all-a-fright in a head&heedless moreorless banshee keen/for/keening. shrill before the sky's death knell noi•some or just can't write-it-off darkest noir over•us•all! or to be exact, that is, of man/woman/chicken/child/everyone. really. so youbetcha any/old/witching/way this omen•amen•ahem of mine assures our sky will will will is falling tumbling twisting howling hellish as in all Kansas gone rumbling under black-cloud vengeance of truly veritas-verily.

ok, eerily also or/and get this: just-adjust-for black fright dust thrown/up in our frail•fray•feckless fey faces like dark death//aces-of-ominous. yup, inspades Dorothy's frightmare of immense downer over/under/all-around. so these scaly-scrambling hen's feet of mine scratching caw-clawings while carrying/crying/ cravening on in my fumble feeble way past every damned/doomed Mcdonalds, Jack-in-the-BoohooedBox, KFSeeeee those damn chicken killers! well, ok we all are box(ed) up/ended in disheveled feather-ruffled time for our very own apocalyptic downtheriver•plucked•soooofucked.

but as usual i'm running around here/everywhere rear/guarding this dumbstate of doom.

# The Mystic in the Basement

*Monica Raymond*

*for Ronald Rowe*

He descends
with me

and carries
up

lumps of
cement

and splintery
old boards

and sweeps
the broken glass

the heaps,
the hoards

of half-finished,
never-read, never-sent

abandoned-
but-not

abandoned-
enough

the torn,
worn

frustrated
garments

fraying, moth-eaten—
when

that is done
he goes

for lunch
and writes

a poem
about the sapphire

crystalline sphere,
split

facings of
the star dome

the infinite
at Hi-Fi

Pizza over a
slice

then goes
to McDonald's

for
coffee.

# Seasoning

*Rachel Woolf*

In spring,
some sprinkle lamb with a seasoning of sea salt, with garlic, bay and rosemary, and spit-roast the meat, for a festive gathering in Genoa or Crete, but I don't; for my gathering is of petals of my damask roses, a gathering of thousands in the uplands of Iran.

In summer,
some swim at leisure in the salt Aegean or play on crowded beach. Such opportunities are not within my reach, as I sort out the figures for the tax to be paid, on export orders for attar of roses, superior grade.

In summer too,
I receive the almonds from my bowing trees, buying sea salt from Brittany, to season a proportion of the crop, which is roasted to perfection and tied up prettily, in bags that I have made from patterned cloth. The remainder of the produce of my sheltered orchard, I shell and grind and sell for use in fine confections.

In autumn,
when the crocus corm, salt of the earth and worth the wait, comes into bloom, I take no rest. The precision extraction of splinters of stigma is an endurance test. The task is barely done, before I weigh and pack and label the insubstantial wisps, which have been set to dry, and seal each little box with wax, red for première qualité, pricing them according to the tax that will be levied and the value of the labour that has gone into the production of every gram of saffron.

In winter,
in Stockholm, some bake saffron bread for the welcoming of visitors. In Brussels, others, when dining in company, proffer pastel-tinted macaroons with after-dinner coffee. In Edinburgh, others still, invite invited guests to drink a dram and nibble salted offerings and cake of brandied fruit with, concealed beneath the icing, a layer of marzipan. In Lombardy, my stigma gild saffron risotto, for those who meet and greet in the restaurants of Milan.

Meanwhile, everywhere, glassy cubes of loukoum waft their rosy perfume, redolent of breathless days of May, bewitching children with their alchemy and getting faces sticky.

Thus the yield my harvest brings will take me to Morocco, where they lay lemons down in salt, to make a piquant condiment, added as ingredient, together with some whispered strands of stigma plucked by my own hands, to suffuse a lamb tagine with taste beyond imagining, renewing bonds with kith and kin.

For the very act of sharing a repast in rich conviviality is, itself, a seasoning, without price and tax-free.

# Rio Hondo Crossroads

*Steve Wing*

# Quick Brew

*Rachel Dacus*

Monday morning's a three-minute brew, a click
at every turn in the kitchen to quicken
the oncoming hour. Fix a rushed breakfast
and down it doing slapdash dance steps,
only to be caught unaware by a sudden splash
of sunlight on pink tiles, how it warms and slows
the ankles back to sultry Sunday's drift.

Still, it's time to run and get the spreadsheet glowing
between bites and steps, to dive into an analytical grid,
square and tuck in diamonds of fact
while surreptitiously opening a blank page
to gleam behind apparent logic.
This one. No warmth here until I lay it in,
but the prodding intellect can't divine
what makes skin leap to sun as soul to music.
Sneak a poem between the cells. Sip an image lightly,
quickly, leaning one shoulder back
toward slower rhythms, while facing
forward and typing smart into the glare.

# Sustenance

An excerpt from *Imaginary Loves*

*Jessamyn Smyth*

I am loved by someone so well that I never doubt it, Bettany says, as the nurse puts the IV into her arm. Do you know what that's like?

This is what it's like, the nurse answers, jabbing unnecessarily, when you refuse to eat.

The nurse's sister died of anorexia.

She is very angry.

Bettany floats in the gray-white haze of zero blood sugar, way down below weakness and well risen to euphoria. Sooner or later, they will leave the room. She will take out the IV. They will come and put it back. She will wait, take it out; a perfection of passive resistance.

He meets me in the middle, she says.

If you take this out again, the nurse answers, you're going into restraints.

Bettany considers the blue-black hair of the nurse. Like raven feathers, she says aloud. What is your name?

Sucking up to me isn't going to help.

I'm not. I want to know your name.

My name doesn't matter, says the nurse. I'm the nurse.

It matters to me, says Bettany.

No, it doesn't, says the nurse. What matters to you is getting a grip on reality.

I have one, Bettany says. I am loved. It feeds me.

The nurse finishes taping the IV, cleans up a line of blood dripped down the girl's emaciated arm. Leave it this time, she says, or restraints. I mean it.

Did I tell you about the letter he sent me?

You can't eat letters, the nurse says.

Oh, yes, says Bettany, rising to one elbow with quaking effort. Yes you can.

---

## The Core of a Woman

*Pia Taavila*

One cold tomato on a white plate.

Taut skin. Beads of moisture.

The bitter stem. Leaves, serrated.

Quartered.

Pulp. Juice.

Suspended seeds.

Waiting to be salted.

# Melons

*Richard Spuler*

I like to believe things are what they are.
Tap on a melon, it tells you it's a melon.
Ripeness resonates, you listen with both ears:
already you can hear it snap and fracture

into pieces that you'll later contemplate, then eat.
The melon will be what it is, nothing more
and nothing less than what it is, and that means
ready to sacrifice itself for a job well done.

Not everything is melons. Not everything will
talk to you, divulging secrets of its seeds,
obliging you to look for fertile ground,
guaranteeing their progression from simple to complex.

No matter which fruit you choose to sample,
you'll sense oblique connections between the simple
and the complex, the hidden kinship that they share.
You'll want to find a melon and go home.

This is no easy task. The field you tend
is bounded on all sides by razor wire.
Your hands know this as a deep, hard fact,
and know that scars, like melons are what they are.

No, not everything is melons. Some fractures
that you'll hear will be your bones. Snapping
and marking painful changes, changes
making you wish that life just went tap-tap.

# Isles and Lakes

Six oatcakes in the forms of isles and lakes

*Alec Finlay*

Alec explains the piece as follows:

"I often work with simple forms and I conceived this piece from my occasional habit of making oatcakes—the outlines always look geographical, often northerly. I chose isles and lakes as the positive and negative, here united in one idiom, and as they are the Romantic destinations par excellence. Some choices were autobiographical, some for the sake of predecessor poets or artists, some for form alone."

The Isles and Lakes are: the Isle of Sado, Walden Pond, Cythera, Aral Sea, White Lake and Derwent Water. Alec leaves it to the reader to guess or imagine which is which. (The original piece won Alec the 2006 International Edible Art Award. Caroline Smith baked the oatcakes here. The Village Bakery commissioned the cutters. Photographs by Alexander Maris.)

Oatmeal became the staple grain of Scotland because it is better suited than wheat to the country's short, wet growing season. It therefore has a long culinary history going back many centuries, so much so that Scotland's ancient universities had a holiday called Meal Monday, to permit students to return to their homes to collect more oats for food.

Scottish oatmeal is created by grinding oats into a coarse powder. Various grades are available depending on the thoroughness of the grinding, including coarse, pin (head) and fine oatmeal. It has many uses, including being the main ingredient of bannocks or oatcakes.

In celebration of Alec's project, and the oatcake, we thought it might be good idea to provide an oatcake recipe, and this one comes with the kind permission of Wendy Harrison at *A Wee Bit of Cooking*, a Scottish food blog:

**Oatcakes**

225g oats
60g whole wheat flour
30g butter
30g lard or vegetable fat
1 tspn salt
1/2 tspn bicarbonate of soda
50 ml boiling water

* Mix together the oats, flour and bi-carb.
* Add the butter and lard and rub together until the fats are incorporated and look like big breadcrumbs (this took the full length of Meatloaf's "Bat Out of Hell" when I last did it).
* Add the boiling water little by little and combine until thick, stiff dough is formed.
* Scatter extra flour and oats on a surface and roll out the dough until 1/2 cm thick (or thinner if you prefer daintier biscuits). Use cutter to cut out shapes.
* Reroll dough and cut again until dough is used up.
* Place shapes on baking tray and bake in 190oC oven for 20-30 mins until brown and crisp around the edges.
* Remove from oven when golden and crisp around the edges.

—Anna Dickie and Pamela Hart, eds.

# The Economic Heart

*Maureen Jivani*

Boris married Maria, the butcher's widow, on a bright day last December. It was a small affair. Although the villagers were respectful of Boris's profession many were still reeling from the butcher's death at thirty-two. He was too young for a heart-attack, although Boris had signed the death certificate himself.

Maria had married the butcher on a chilly day last May. It was a grand affair. The ladies adored the butcher for his nutritious sweet sausages and the men were grateful for his un-relenting generosity during the recession. Women had deprived their families of breakfast eggs for months, in order to present the happy couple with a giant cake. Men had gone willingly without ale for a week.

On the night of their honeymoon, the butcher urged his young wife to consider starting a family. Maria pulled the candlewick bedspread over her shoulders and looked at him with such child-like intensity that he felt ashamed.

The next day Maria cut her hair short, locked away her treasured make-up and took to wearing ankle socks. The butcher came back that evening to no supper, and finding her curled on the sofa like a stray kitten, gasped, 'My god Maria!'

When Boris arrived and had thoroughly examined Maria in the privacy of the marital bed, he reassured the butcher that 'such regressions into childhood were not uncommon in young brides,' and 'that Maria needed only daily counselling sessions with him to resolve the matter.' The butcher wept as Boris shrugged and said, 'six months.'

After the first session Maria improved. She discarded the socks, glossed her lips, and her cheeks took on a healthy glow. She began to cook her husband the hearty meals she had promised before they were married, and at night she would whisper 'soon, my love, soon.'

# Pliant de Voyage; Objects of Desire

*Alex Cigale*

After the notebooks of Marcel Duchamp

> *"The penalty consists*
> *in 'cutting the pane',*
> *in feeling regret*
> *just as soon as the*
> *article's possession*
> *is consummated."*

Many readymades
            suggest a body,
parts of the body,
            bodily functions,
erotic promise,
            stand-ins for body,
consumers seduced
            into a purchase.

Sexuality is
            like window shopping.
So ... endow objects
            with human desires:
the leering grin of
            the bathroom faucet,
faces everywhere,
            the world eroticized.

Design devices
            for things personal,
such as teeth, eyes, breath.
                        Violate aversion.
Live life on credit,
            prophecy fulfilled,
certain of future worth,
                        and free to create.

Frustrate reading.
            Upset expectations.

# Evening

*Angela Koh*

Street lamps flicker on and I'm the last to head home.
Dusk settles over the bare parking lot.

The cold pierces the skin like a syringe to a girl's arm,
a man in Burma holds her as the liquid sinks into her flesh.

I shift the stack of papers I'm holding and there is no point
in working late. The girl prays, her eyes wide and white.

The tip of my key, jamming into the car lock, fits in.
The man ties ropes around the girl's wrist to the bed post.

Enough to keep her heart pulsing to find a vein;
she will be awake for a few more hours.

Begging for sleep, she will see a pike of lust
stretch the soul out of her body. I see the sky.

The first drops of rain slide down the windshield.
The girl begins to hum like the start of the engine.

# Then Again: In Meditation on Ruskin's *Stones of Venice*

*Joanne Hudson*


Then again, you are made of triangles
Your eyes, lips, cheeks all joined in harmony
Your stance, a point of geometry
Isoscelism is your creed and scale

My body's made of circles all a tangle
Circular logic travels well on me
Both body and thought housing holes to scry
Both curving softly into folds, no angle

Inside a triangle the circle stays put
While the triangle's encompassed dutiful
Within the circle's circumference; *He spoke*

*of the hibiscus sitting in a circle*
*in a triangular relief,* with soot
Building on the door's lintel in New York

# Math Tutor

*Pia Taavila*

Today I tire of abstract lectures,
trigonometry's equations,
the theory of topology.

Put away your textbook.
Assess the addition of our absolute
values. Multiply the factors.

Kiss me. Until we test,
it's all hypothesis. Gather data.
Calculate initial results.

Kiss me again, exponentially.
Above its x/y axis,
let me graph your parabola's arc.

If the plot points fail,
we can go back to zero.
Meet me in the lab of love.

# Visual Economy

*Anne Morrison Smyth*

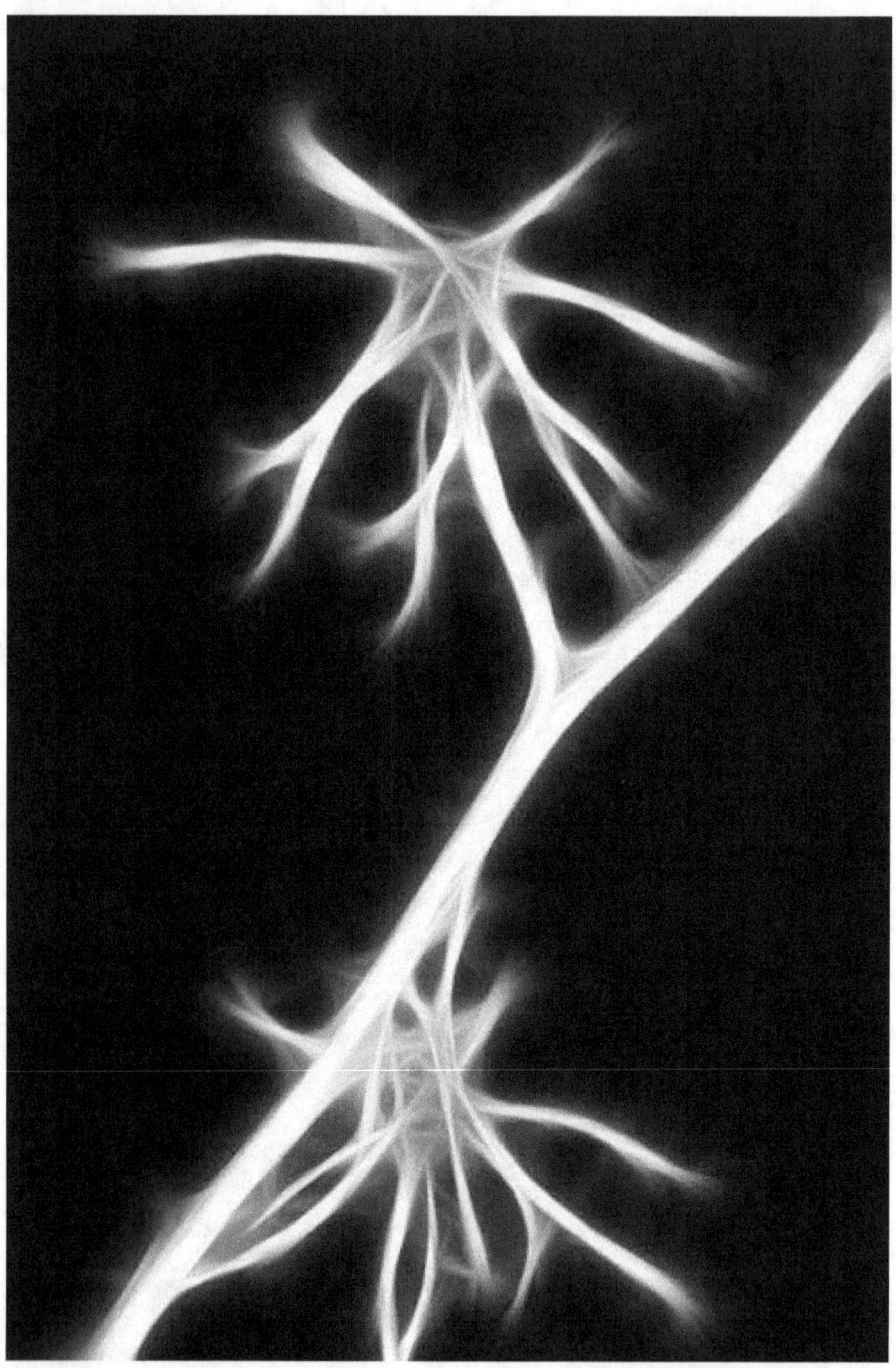

# The Economy of Porn

*Maureen Jivani*

She voices no words
for her long absence,
her wasted frame

the time it takes
to make her face,
to fix her hair

and reach the set
where she strips
to the waist,

pours molasses
over her breast
as the camera films

the inevitable spill
to the ribs
before fading to black.

## Post-Coital

*Eileen R. Tabios*

Light          sweet          crude

```
        d
      e
    k
   a
  e
 p
```

```
          f
        e
          l
            l
```

"to settle at $44.51 a barrel on the New York Mercantile Exchange."
It was Paris. But in Texas.

## Truck Song, You and I

*Gregory Stapp*

The radio is hobbled in this mottled blue truck with its touches of cancerous rust,

the antenna a broken stub,

but the truck sings a 200,000 mile tune. Between muffler sputters and engine knocks,

who needs Elvis or Cheryl Crow?

The tire's rhythmic thrumming, the periodic squeak, keep us humming into the night.

Lying in the bed at the hilltop,

we wonder who waits for the stars to burn out? The fuel gauge shows empty,

it always does,

and the odometer is unreliable. On the way home you start to worry

about how much farther we can go.

# Space Walk

*Glenda Bailey-Mershon*

At night, Reina played among the stars.

She rose from her pillow, gliding up and up, one arm outstretched, as the Earth spun into a small ball below. Inevitably, she bumped into a speeding comet, pulled herself up and perched on it, as on a black velvet throne, surveying the planets rolling away like glass marbles into the field of space. When she tired of the views passing before her, she skipped onto other heavenly objects—asteroids, moons big and small, unidentified bits of space junk of unknown origin—until she sighted the phenomena she most loved: giant, spinning galaxies, great milky spills of stars across the horizon-less void.

Her days unfurled in stark contrast to her nights. She awoke in her bed to rise and dress in stained shirts and shorts, took the bus to where she crawled on her knees across someone else's kitchen floor, sodden cloth in hand, crunchy cereal and cracker crumbs prickling her fleshy limbs. Under her absentminded gaze, load after load of soiled clothes turned spotless.

Then she ran home for her nightly adventures. For slow leaps through universes rushing like amusement park rides, one into another. In some of those universes she was a child again. Her father blew dandelion fluff with great gusts of his stubbly cheeks, as Reina leapt to catch it. In others, she was someone she had not yet been: a woman with an explorer's audacious smile, diving through blazing wormholes, stardust billowing around her like sheets on a line.

So many Reinas, so many ways to travel.

One night, as Reina rested on Saturn's innermost ring, where she had been watching gases rush like colored streamers across the planet's face, she felt a moving presence. She peered behind her. No one. Yet, still, a ripple trailed across her outer limits, mass in motion, like a cool wave. Benign? Uncertain, but she thought … probably, yes. A brief pause, and the other moved deliberately, slowly, away, a fish swishing through deep water.

The next day, Reina stood at the curbside market, flexing her aching shoulders and considering lunch, when she perceived someone watching her. A big, blowzy lady had swept awry a tower of limes as she passed, intent on peaches. Behind her, the shopkeeper regarded Reina with a shy smile, as he scooped up green orbs and placed them neatly back in pyramids. Reina loved limes, their cool tartness like saucy tongues. She reached for one. Her hand brushed the shopkeeper's hand. A familiar tug.

"You like space travel?" she blurted. A statement to him, a question to herself. Could she really recognize that same cool fingering she had felt during her space walk?

"You know Saturn?" she asked in wonder.

"I love Saturn," he replied. "Those colored streams, that prickly ring thing, like a shower of ice sparks. Love it." His long, thin fingers picked up an orange. The other hand plunged into cold crystals underneath a case of salmon. He drew forth a thin, sparkling band of ice, then sent it all in orbit around the two of them, the zeroth law of thermodynamics circling right before her eyes.

Thus, Reina met her Max. Without hesitation, she stepped into his world, learned to haggle for prices with truck farmers, who pulled from their vans boxes of fruits and vegetables, burning colorful and explosive, like supernovas, like blue and red dwarfs, like comets spraying green tendrils into the city's desultory air.

Reina loved stacking produce, feeling the charged textures, the energy potential of each one. Some of their customers saw it, this bright rush of chlorophyll, of pungent atoms, at once sustenance and decay. They smiled dreamily while handing over their cash, perhaps thinking of gleaming particles flowing through their bloodstreams. Others thrust money at the shopkeepers, heads and eyes down, ignoring warm smiles, grasping their purchases as if squelching life within their grip.

At night, Max amused her by slicing dinner ingredients as they floated across the kitchen, his knife strewing peels of zucchini, chunks of carrots, zests of lemon through steamy currents, over bubbling pots. Together, they slept beneath swirls of cosmic dust and wandered through distant star fields. Each morning, as they opened the store's front gates, brilliant eggplants and celery rushed to meet them, like bit players in a big top show.

"So many universes," Reina murmured one day, when Venus clung to the horizon.

"Yes, light years and light years to explore," replied Max. After glancing around to ensure they were alone, he balanced a watermelon on his fingertip, tossed kumquats into a wide pattern around it. Reina swelled with possibility. With a twirl of her wrist, she sent strawberries swirling from their green plastic cages to dash among the orange balls, surprising Max, astounding herself!

A customer arrived with a sudden clash of bells above the door, creating a momentary bobble in their midst. Reina thought, "Freeze time," and saw the fruits come to a sudden halt, undetected by the man with the briefcase, who quickly chose an apple and a banana from the baskets by the register. As she lifted her hand to return his change, she saw the star stuff trailing from her own fingertips. At that moment, she acknowledged a quiver deep inside herself, saw the logical extension of her relationship with Max.

"There's been an energy exchange," she whispered, rubbing her swelling belly.

"A conversion, something new," he suggested.

"What next?" they asked as one. And enjoyed not knowing the answer.

People who stepped through their door saw they had entered a unified state. At night, Reina and Max linked arms, rose, back to back, swimmers in the nightscape, feeling the fit of blade to blade, their own zygotic matter immersed in light. The earth, with its cacophony of crashing cars, its mounds of dirty laundry, souls trudging dejectedly from work to home and back, became a shining, glittering puzzle in their sky. New universes called.

# blue Raleigh

*Kay McKenzie Cooke*

Loose-mudguard rattle, sixties'
teal and white
and your faithful charger
on through the seventies
and eighties.

The only thing it guzzled,
your energy. One day
in the nineties
just before you finally
dump it,

the boys and I spot it in town
outside your work, parked
in its usual bike rack,
a donkey in a stable
of mountain-bike

thoroughbreds;
an object of ridicule
and their shame.
Already they'd forgotten
the once-familiar kerklunk

over our driveway's kerb,
the handbrake's strangled screech
outside the front door,
those announcements
that you'd arrived

home from work
their cue
to hurl their small bodies
headlong
into your handlebar arms.

# Critical Mass, Vancouver

*Alan Girling*

There was no way to determine
the criticality of the mass
of happy, hooting cyclists
kinetic on the downtown street
on the last Friday of April,
but one guy at the corner
who had waited too long
in his silver suit
to cross that street
felt compelled
to flip them all the bird,
as though the chain reaction
they were creating
would reach him
eventually—
the fallout of two-wheelers
an affront to his muscle
car life.

Meanwhile, and in contrast,
the line of customers waiting
at the Japa-Dog stand on the corner
was growing exponentially—
it was, for the moment,
a new equilibrium.

# Collective

*Kristin Berkey-Abbott*

At first his requests seem
reasonable. He wants to learn
to sew. He wants no stain
of sweatshops on his clothes.
He wants a seamless
ethical life, no frayed
edges of hypocrisy.

At first, we have fun.
Of course, I'd always dreamed
of doing this with a daughter,
but I'll settle for sewing with my son.
He's been a bit adrift.
It's good to see him settle
into a hobby.

But then he wants to know
who made the cloth,
and all our efforts unravel.
So hard to live an upright life
with all one's values in alignment.

He decides there's nothing to be
done but to raise his own goats and sheep,
and soon he attracts like-minded pilgrims.

They've moved out to the country
where they raise organic vegetables.
There's a homebaked bread collective
and a vineyard and winery,
and, of course, cruelty-free cloth
and clothes of Christian design.
They weave, and break bread together,
and pray without ceasing.

# Year Abroad Room and Board

*Merry Speece*

piece of china
called a boat
my heart in it

## Trickle-Up

*William Sea*

In New York,
I would walk down
three flights of stairs
and buy cigarettes from
Key Food.

I would fancy myself
melancholy, meaningful,
poetic, and would pay cash.
I scoffed at the stolid
Manhattan banks, their
spires scratching the ancient sky.

Now, at a Flying J in Abilene,
I only yawn and swipe my card,
noticing my wrist is
pale where my watch was,
and my knuckles are
sharp and pink, and I am
growing older. I take
the receipt, and think

somehow, all I have spent
is floating now, slowly
and silently as smoke,
until it reaches the exact same place.

# How Appurtenances Are Made Sacred

*Alex Cigale*

Her long silk robes and knitted caftans doused—
torn to shreds, soaked in gasoline, and set ablaze—
the shattered remains of her guitars tossed
on the burning rags, her entire household,

the caravan's contents, her cherished possessions—
pots and pans, white lace shawls, brass candlesticks—
were burned and both her beloved horses shot.
Sleep had deceived Ulla; her knife would not sing.

Ulla, the old gypsy queen, has passed on.
She will need her possessions in the afterlife.
No one should be sent off to the spirit world
without their things. All wealth is "sad money."

Only in death is there pleasure without spend.
We dressed Ulla as for her wedding day.

# Frui

*Angela Koh*

Mom always loved the rain. She loved the sharp edges of the stones
washed with it. Because she liked things clean.

It cleans every alley, she said.
God must like things clean. She was sure of this

more than the broken zippers
and the washed take-out boxes she saved in the pantry.

She loved to bleed.
Maybe she finally sensed God's cleaning in it.

# A Rainy Day

*Claire Quigley*

# A Different Planet

*Ray Templeton*

A sudden descent of mist
obscures a view of the sea;
there's a small rise in the price of cream.
Tonight the train was late:
frustration turned to rage.
The final over-ran, delayed the news:
all much the same old stuff.

# Missing

*Kristin Berkey-Abbott*

She spent her childhood surrounded
by the missing.
Kidnapped children peered out from milk
cartons, heiresses vanished, then reappeared
in shaky surveillance tapes. Shadowy
foreign governments seized civilians
and held them for years, and terrorists
of all stripes did the same.

She thinks of those Iranian hostages,
held in their workplace, walled
up for over a year. Some evenings,
she feels like a captive
herself, although no scruffy terrorist
holds her at gunpoint, just the shapeless
terrors of bankruptcy and a job hunt at midlife.

She spent half her life expecting to be seized,
but she did not expect so many selves
to be sacrificed. She used to greet
the dawn by logging long runs.
Now she watches the sun rise over jammed cars
on the morning commute.
She used to plant a garden large enough to feed
her family for a season.
Now she picks up a quick meal where she can
or settles for microwaved popcorn.
She used to paint sprawling canvases
that dreamt visions of a new world,
but now she tends to files and forms.
She used to hike through strange parts of the globe.
Now her vacation days, unused, evaporate
at the end of the fiscal year.

# Doing My Part

*Kate Irving*

Today it's a long way to the river
dragging two large boxes
I don't remember buying
but addressed to me, all right.
I drop them over the railing knowing
a splash will billow sure as night
closes the mall, sure as lambs
follow tails through the gate
the way hope limped into this century
from the last, the one I learned by,
now flown like a gull's cry over two boxes
moving down river who knows where. Maybe
halfway across the world they'll find castaways
grateful for toasters, cell phones,
tall skim lattes, a case of the blues;
something they can really use.

# The Bookmark

*Russell Helms*

The small square letter addressed to Aunt Bev and Uncle Steve—Don uses it as a bookmark. The house is 28 years old and looks new inside. Don, Lori and their girls live there now.

\*

When Steve decided to rip up the carpet, upstairs and down, he didn't ask Bev. He just did it. An engineer by trade, Steve was precise and it took him nine months of weekends to lay 2,100 square feet of hard maple flooring. Bev spent a lot of time outdoors, weary of the mess.

When Don and Lori and the girls came over with their real estate agent to meet the Stovers, Steve worshiped his gorgeous hardwood floors and bragged endlessly on the wood-slat shades in the study. Here, let me show you, he said to Don. You just pull 'em down by the bottom and it stays. They don't make 'em anymore. You can't buy these anymore. The girls raced through the house.

The central vacuum was less than five years old, same as the hardwood floors. Steve loved the central vacuum. He showed Lori how to insert the hose in the wall and a quiet but massive suction followed. Bev slipped in and out of the house. The girls argued over the bedroom with the pink carpet.

Steve made sure that Don noticed the new roof, just about five years old he said. They were composite shingles, applied according to the manufacturer's instructions. The roofers take shortcuts, he said. The composite shingles, he pointed to the roof, see how they lay, how they kind of look like they're slightly lifted, that's texture he said, shows they were nailed down right. Bev carried picture frames to a Volvo station wagon.

You guys have any kids? asked Don. Steve laughed and said, Nope.

Sara, the oldest, convinced Patty to take the room with the blue carpet. It had a better view and a bigger closet. Bev frowned. She'd thought that herself for years.

The sun was bright that day, but a cold wind made standing outside looking at the roof less fun than it should have been. And then Steve launched into a rapture about the vinyl siding. Don didn't care for vinyl siding and wondered what was hiding underneath. But it looked good—probably the tightest, nicest looking siding job he had ever seen. Steve assured them the siding was top grade, overkill he said, and like the relatively new garage doors, hurricane proof.

Bev put a black clock radio in the backseat of the Volvo and walked up behind Steve. He ignored her, talking up the brass doorknobs in the house, how they were solid brass, how he hated to leave them because they were so nice.

Back inside to see the custom lights in the living room, Sara pushed Patty across the bare floor on a wooden barstool. Steve and Bev went blank.

We're sorry, said Lori.

# We Never Talk Anymore

*Meredith Trede*

Let's prepare a list of topics, we make
our living listening and talking—

turn the dinner table into Chautauqua.
We don't do jokes, dreams always

fall flat in retelling, we think we know
all about us. I'm not allowed

to criticize your kids and I'm sure
you've nothing to say about mine. Truth,

beauty, how about those Yankees,
land on politics and we're preaching

to the choir, work went well, a good day,
nice piece of fish, please pass me

some olives. Wine? There is much to be said
for long-coupled companionate silence.

# An Economical Fairytale

*Kelsey Blair*

Princess Eileen once lived.[1] She sat in a room of neutral hues.[2] Unlike her counterparts, who twiddled their thumbs in giant towers, grew their hair out, or experienced great hardships, Princess Eileen went to school. She buried her nose in books and ambition.[3] She studied free trade, and the stock market. She also studied art, deciding all concepts were the same level of abstraction. It was all a bit of a slog, the testing, the memorization, but Princess Eileen didn't have a choice. In truth, she too was a lady in waiting. A Prince[4] was supposed to be part of her story.

Prince dreamt of saving, but spent most of his time looking at clouds.[5]

"I hate my job," said Prince one day.

Princess Eileen said, "Well, why not find a new one?"[6]

The prince gasped, "Have you seen the economy lately?"

The princess hadn't.[7] "What's it like? The Economy?"

"Like a dragon, only it can be prettier."

"Do you like pretty things?"

"Only if they stay that way."[8]

He was supposed to save her. In fact, he was supposed to have saved her three years prior, but, at the time, he'd been too busy with his profits. Then, he'd been rather swept up in his new-found love of squash. Six months ago, it was simply impossible to help ease Princess Eileen's need for new colour coordination because he was trying to focus more on fixing his bad habits.[9]

She tilted her head to the side, "Are you ever going to save me?"

"Of course!" said Prince, standing up full force, getting a head rush, and quickly sitting back down.

Princess Eileen titled her head further to the side, getting up slowly and taking a walk of the castle.[10]

In the forest, Princess Eileen ran into a wise person.[11]

This person spoke eloquently on many subjects. "I, too, used to be royal."[12]

"How did you end up here?"[13]

In listening, the princess learned a lesson.[14]

She returned to the castle and went rummaging through the garage.

Days turned to weeks, which turned to months. Princess Eileen went back into the castle, a dash of red along her forearm. While skipping through the hallway, she ran into Prince.

"I am going to save you," he said bravely.

Princess Eileen tilted her head at him again.

"Eventually," he mumbled, "have you been out there lately? Things are crashing. Numbers falling from the sky. Executives too."

"I have been out there. The sky wasn't falling," she responded simply, "Oh, and I no longer need saving."

"What?"

"If it's not the economy, it'll be an evil witch."

"Witches are difficult to deal with. They possess all sorts of powers. Dark powers. Is that blood on your arm?"

"No, it's paint. I've been redecorating. My tower was quite drab. I've decided to become a designer."

"You're supposed to be the decoration."

"No, I'm supposed to be saved, but you aren't coming."

"Well, I mean the economy."

"Yes, the economy, the witches, the dragons. Regardless … I don't need saving. I do however need more paint."

So ends the story.[15]

NOTES

1. For the sake of space, time and context are irrelevant. Safe to say she lived, or is living; verb tense is of no matter.

2. Setting. It should be inferred her life was dull, boring, and in need of help. No one who paints a room "cream" is filled with passion.

3. Character traits which demonstrate Princess Eileen's desperate state: education is, as we all know, exceptionally dangerous for the rich. It is also dangerous for the poor, but far less accessible.

4. Despite his generic title, the Prince is very important; hence, capitalization. Also, Prince and Princess Eileen are not related. It's very difficult to root for incest.

5. Conflict: Prince vs. Princess. Unlike Princess vs. Evil Stepmother, all creatures, including excessively small persons, horses with horns, and inanimate objects with the power of speech will be useless to advancing the plot. There is no room for comic relief here. Even very witty relief.

6. She raised her eyes from the large book she was reading and tried to flip her hair. It was an action she didn't practice often. Needless to say, it went badly, and Prince furrowed his brow in a confused way. As has been noted, Prince wasn't very bright.

7. Princesses are consistently badly acquainted with their enemies. Some sort of genetic flaw?

8. This answer is unfitting. Clearly, the Prince had things to learn. There isn't time for that here, but the record notes: maturation needed.

9. A pattern has formed. Lengthy, but necessary, like a long journey.

10. Clearly, no room for descriptors. However, safe to say, the grounds were large and lush. The forest, located near the back gate was rarely attended to. Past the gate, which was made of a kind of steel so strong it was luminous, were trees. "Trees" is a bad descriptor, suggesting something mundane, found on street corners and window sills. These plants manage to create space while also seeming to hug anyone who enters them.  It is a place children dream of getting lost in, full of bright coloured insects and crickets that seem to sing instead of chirp. Not that any of this is relevant.

11. For the sake of equality, the person will not be gendered. For the sake of discrimination, the person will not be a peasant or old. Class and age are not factors here.

12. Princess Eileen had met one other being who claimed to be royal. She'd never since like the taste of frog legs.

13. The story, was, of course, long, winding, and only moderately exciting to listeners.

14. This is ever so important. You are supposed to learn this lesson too. Did you?

15. Normally, there would be a review of the moral, but space is not permitting. For reassurance sake, Princess Eileen did live, even relatively happily. She made a business for herself, painting castles, saving others from unsatisfactory colours. She waited for no one.

# An Economy of Language

*James Brush*

They wouldn't even pay him off in pennies,
said his poems wandered far too long:

too many synthesaurus additives,
too many old growth words chopped down.

Strapped him to an ankle monitor
that somehow read his thoughts,

buzzed all night when he tried to sleep
and garnished away his dreams.

Hollow-eyed and somber silent, now,
he hoards his words in a coffee can

buried out back beneath the pine, planted
in days when all the things had many names.

Sometimes he spreads his words out,
arranging them in patterns on the grass,

building shapes of presidents and snakes
before burying them in the earth again,

hidden from the hungry mouths of singers,
linguists and bright-eyed myna birds.

# New Poem Breathing

*Tom Sheehan*

Curry a new poem
with a wire brush

toss vanity aside
when you dare to

hit it two or more swipes
with the same scrub brush

your mother kept the kitchen
clean with, drag with a fine tooth comb

the kind she sought out nits
with when school was overrun

the way ant hordes might come
yet, fire ants from Brazil's interior

the Amazon bone-dry
old wells besieged

silence the final
architect

# blown by the wind

*Michael Aanji Crowley*

# My Lady Copia

*M. V. Montgomery*

Perhaps because I can get so tongue-tied, I am not naturally economical in writing. *Cut half of what you write,* advises my father, who is something of a raconteur. *Drop your last paragraph to avoid appearing argumentative,* counsels my lawyer, himself a gladiator. True, E.B. White held a good school. The English language is naturally redundant: "to be" constructions, excessive nominalizations, clichés—all deservedly banished from the Republic of Letters. Adjectives and figures of speech: never use when an action word will do. And by god, throw away your thesaurus.

It is always surprising, though, when the Occam's Razor falls on poetry: *We cannot consider poems of more than twenty lines. We ask that you kindly sum things up and get to the point.* Of course the poem itself may have been the point: the vent, the spill, the tendril, the brave search party sent out after other words. (Pardon my pleonasm.) The safest course is to unloose the diction only when it's certain to seem appropriate. A eulogy? You can get away with that sort of thing. Trash-talking with friends? Of course you must play that game. An affectionate letter? Even those I have been encouraged to tone down. Don't pontificate, don't come on too strong, don't jinx things with your exuberance. So I end here. It is, as they say, a wrap. *Ad Finem. Vale.*

# A 92-Degree Day

*Don Skiles and Peter Cherches*

"Look," Mullins said—we were by that time crossing the very busy and wide intersection at Van Ness and Market Streets, a trolley clunking and wheezing by us, cars speeding in all directions, like pinballs gone berserk—"I don't know what it means. You understand me? I'm a writer, and if I don't write, I don't feel good. You know, I read somewhere Dylan said if he didn't work he didn't feel good."

"Oh?" I said, in an uninflected tone befitting the sheer banality.

He went on. "I suspect it's that way with a lot of writers. I mean, you can't do much with it, can you? Maybe a job teaching in a two-bit college. A sinecure."

He said the word contemptuously. We had reached the other side of the street in one piece, and I found I was dusting myself off, literally. It was a brutally hot day for San Francisco. The illuminated, flashing thermometer on the side of the bank building read "92." I mopped my brow, my dripping wet, uncharacteristically so for San Francisco, brow.

"God! There are too many damn writers in this town," he said. "I bet you every fifth person we've passed today is some kind of writer. Or wants to be." He turned to me. "Why is that?"

I had no answer. Instead I thought about my first sinecure.

It was 1967 and I was hired on the telephone, wham, bam, interview and job offer in under fifteen minutes, that's how it was back then. My call came early in the morning, around 8:15 San Francisco time, but it was 10:15 out there in the Midwest. I had just completed my masters at San Francisco State, which at the time had one of the most respected English faculties in the country. And it was in San Francisco, damn it, the adopted home I had fallen in love with.

Well, I found myself in September of 1967 living in a new apartment on the middle floor of a three-story concrete apartment building in a godforsaken university town in the northern Midwest, a town whose main distinction was that barbed wire had been invented there. The mansion of the inventor had become a museum, dually honoring the man's life and his greatest achievement.

It didn't last very long, that first sinecure in the town with the barbed-wire museum. One year. Nine months, actually, and those nine months were the longest year of my life, and the winter the coldest.

After that, a short stint at a small college in Pennsylvania, in a not-unpleasant town, and this one with a museum dedicated to Little League baseball. But I wasn't cut out for two-bit sinecures, I guess, and I returned to San Francisco where I worked a succession of jobs over the years, some good, some bad, some awful. Eventually, though it took quite a number of years, I found my way back into teaching, and without leaving the Bay Area. In all that time I had never quit writing.

"I don't know," I told Mullins, finally, without inflection, as I mopped my brow again, a Sisyphean task, it seemed, especially in San Francisco.

# 401(k)

*Ed Higgins*

Icarus-like nearing the sun
contrail streak
falling

      fa
         ll
           in
              g
waxed wings
me
   lt
     in
       g
wildly
in the grieving sky.

# Balance

*Anne Connolly*

Are you able to catch that blackbird's song?

You know fine well my higher hearing's gone—
controlled explosions and pneumatic drills.

So I try to tune him first to soaring trills
then see-saw notes of warning as the cat
invisibles his predatory self in under-
growth; how the molasses of his song
meanders nightfall when the threat moves on.

Hey look! A golden eagle way up there!

No chance hawk-eye! Marking jotters till dawn.
You know I'm blinder than a cricket ball.

And with his own precision he gives me sun
on the edge of a wind-span throttled back sweet
to find ungainly land in the lee of morning
while I slit my eyes to hear the young call.

## Pearl, Lantern

*Merry Speece*

lovelessness
broken necklace
the Asian markets
opening lower
the fall
the fall of
the American dol-
lar
a light in China
Americans with pearl vision
as American as mini pearls
seed pearl
seed money and seed purse
plant case for the plant seed
it looks like a paper lantern

# Recessional

*Colin Will*

Everyone's on promotions now—
bogof, twofers, reduced for quick sale.

It's what we war babies always did—
scoured for bargains, secreted pleasures.

An inheritance of thrift became habit,
even in later soppy days of plenty.

I splurge on things never then imagined—
books, music, a house to hold all,

education for the children, ambitions
grafted on totipotent lives, a plastic future.

# Recession: A User's Guide

*Nathan Moore*

Your outlook should become more depressed over
the budget. If banks implode, search for some anodyne
that could ease forgetfulness. As for your television,
leave it in your front yard until a neighbor comes to argue
its price. Avoid paying for small items—especially
those that are not behind glass. In the meantime,
anonymous benefactors may offer you loans via the Internet.
Make sure your car is easy to hide and your name is fake.

\*

Your anguish should become more apparent over the telephone.
If collections calls, ask for flexible managers who can learn
to fuck themselves. As for your microwave, store it in your garage
until a neighbor comes to cook a burrito. Avoid
making payments—especially those that are not life threatening.
In the meantime, strangers may mysteriously eat your money
via the Internet. Make sure your hair is combed and your identity
is somewhat intact.

\*

Your children should become savvier about the market.
If jobs open in coal mining or textiles, it could lead to steady
income. As for your credit rating, employed dependants
guarantee a high score. Avoid selling your children
outright—especially those that are not unskilled.
In the meantime, reproduction may bring you a decent
profit via the birth canal. Make sure your calendar is planned
and your wallet is open.

\*

Your expectations should become more yielding over the years.
If standards relent, look for sleeping arrangements
that could lead to someone's basement. As for your hope,
burn it for warmth until the neighbor comes by with kerosene.
Avoid math problems—especially those that are not coin-related.
In the meantime, your desire for religious salvation through costumed oath
and strange prophecy may be satisfied via the Internet. Make sure your robe
is clean and your doubt suspended.

# Economies

*Monica Raymond*

This must happen
after death: the gold

out of the teeth,
liver broiled instantly,

but the loins smoked and saved
for the long journey.

This must happen:
the heart, wrought solid,

kept for a grinding stone,
crescents of nails

filed clean for amulets.
What falls down

must fall down, but we take
what we need.

We try to use
all that's left.

Sinew for harp strings,
scrimshaw from the long bones,

retina caged
and set singing.

# cupboard's bare

*Michael Aanji Crowley*

# Notes on the Contributors

*(Includes contributors of audio tracks and a video not represented in this print editon. More detailed bios of all contributors are available at the website.)*

**Holly Anderson's** poetry and prose have appeared in several anthologies, and her lyrics can be heard on a number of albums. She's also created limited edition books that are held by major art library collections.

**Glenda Bailey-Mershon** is a member of the Nation of the Four Winds: Romani, Cherokee, Catawba, African, Scottish and Welsh, and knows a thing or two about scattering, whether rosebuds or funds. She's working on a novel about Southern women.

**Caroline Beasley-Baker** is a visual artist who frequently uses words/poems in her work. Her poems and paintings have been published widely and singer-songwriter Peg Simone recorded Beasley-Baker's poem "Trifle and Refrain (I Sang the Stars)" for her album released in 2009.

**Kristin Berkey-Abbott** has published in many journals and currently serves as Assistant Chair of the General Education department at the Art Institute of Ft. Lauderdale. She keeps a poetry blog, a theology blog, and a website.

**Kelsey Blair** is an emerging writer pursuing her masters degree at the University of Toronto. She writes, "If I could choose any method of payment other than money, I'd go with a pound of fresh, seasonal strawberries per word."

**Irene Brown** lives in Edinburgh and has published in a variety of media, including the *Burns Chronicle*. Her chapbook entitled *Glass Slippers* was published in 2009 by Calder Wood Press.

**James Brush** is a writer and an English teacher at a juvenile correctional facility in Austin, Texas. He has published poems and essays and his first novel, *A Place Without a Postcard*, was released in 2003.

**Peter Cherches** has recently developed a passion for finishing other writers' unfinished and abandoned works. He writes about food, travel and the writing life at his blog.

**Alex Cigale** has been published extensively. Some of his translations from the Russian can be found in *Crossing Centuries: the New Generation in Russian Poetry*. He was born in Chernovtsy, Ukraine and lives in New York City.

**Anne Connolly** is from the North of Ireland but currently lives in Edinburgh. Her pamphlet, *Downside Up*, was published last year by Calder Wood Press and many of the poems in it reflect the people, places, and politics of Ireland.

Over the last twenty years many of **Kay McKenzie Cooke**'s poems have been published in literary magazines and included in anthologies. Her poetry book, *Feeding the Dogs*, won the Jessie McKay prize for the Best First Book of Poetry awarded at the New Zealand Book Awards in 2003.

**Michael Aanji Crowley** has a half-dozen galleries of his work online at AMP.

**Stacy Elaine Dacheux** lives in Los Angeles. Her visual work can be found gracing the covers of small press publications and online at her website. She is also a writer and some-time journalist.

**Rachel Dacus** has written three books of poetry and she is a contributing editor for *Umbrella*. She resides in the San Francisco Bay Area.

**Anna Dickie**, one of the two co-editors of this issue, is a photographer and poet based in East Lothian, Scotland. In the last three years she's won or been short-listed in a number of competitions, including having a shot hung in the Scottish Parliament as part of a touring exhibition on the theme of coastal erosion.

**Susan Donnelly** is the author of three books of poetry. Her poems have appeared in *Poetry*, *The New Yorker*, *Prairie Schooner*, and elsewhere. She lives, writes, and teaches poetry in Cambridge, Massachusetts.

**Karyn Eisler** has appeared in *BluePrintReview* and *Geist*. She holds a PhD in sociology and teaches at Langara College. She lives in Vancouver, Canada.

**Alec Finlay** is an artist, poet, and publisher. Born in Scotland in 1966, he now lives in the Northeast of England, in Byker (Newcastle upon Tyne).

**Rachel Fox** grew up in the north of England but has lived in Angus, Scotland since 2002. She has a book of poems, *More about the Song* (Crowd-pleasers Press 2008), a website, and a blog.

**Alan Girling** has written short fiction and has had a play produced. He now focuses on poetry. He writes in Richmond, British Columbia.

**Wendy Harrison** from *A Wee Bit of Cooking* blog is a teacher living in the Highlands of Scotland. She loves growing, cooking and eating food!

**Pamela Hart,** one of the two co-editors of this issue, is a former journalist. Her chapbook, *The End of the Body,* was recently published by toadlily press. She is writer in residence at the Katonah Museum of Art and teaches writing at Long Island University's Graduate School of Education.

**Russell Helms** is a creative writing student at Eastern Kentucky University (EKU). He has published a variety of poems and is the author of several outdoor guides. He is the fiction editor for *Jelly Bucket*, the journal of the Creative Writing Program at EKU.

**Ed Higgins**' poems have been published widely. He and his wife live on a small farm in Yamhill, Oregon where they care for a menagerie of animals including a Manx barn cat named Velcro.

**Joanne Hudson**'s plays have been produced at many theatres across the U.S. She holds an MFA in playwriting from Columbia University and received the Fulbright in 2008 to research and write a play in Iceland. She thanks qarrtsiluni for being the first to publish her poetry.

**Kate Irving** began writing early but went on hiatus for a career in music as a songwriter and studio singer. Her work has appeared in *BigCityLit* and *Press 1* and has been broadcast on WBAI. A native New Yorker, she still lives there.

**Maureen Jivani** has an MPhil in writing from the University Of Glamorgan. She has been published widely in U.K. magazines and journals, and her first collection is forthcoming from Mulfran Press.

**Angela Koh** is a new, up-and-coming writer from California. She is a poet, journalist, linguist, and newbie blogger.

**Dorothee Lang** edits the *BluePrintReview*, an experimental online journal, and is currently into collaborative projects. Her work has appeared in numerous publications.

**Rob A. Mackenzie** lives in Edinburgh, Scotland. His first collection of poetry is *The Opposite of Cabbage*, published by Salt. He blogs at *Surroundings*.

**Robert Mellin** is an architect and professor of architecture at McGill University in Montreal. His book *Tilting: House Launching, Slide Hauling, Potato Trenching, and Other Tales from a Newfoundland Fishing Village* won the Winterset Literary Award in 2003.

**M.V. Montgomery** is a professor teaching in the Atlanta area whose work has appeared recently in *Conversation Poetry Quarterly* and *Tangent Literary Arts Magazine*.

**Nathan Moore** spent seven years working full-time in a photograph factory while getting an undergraduate degree in English literature at Clarion University in Clarion, Penn. Nathan shares his writing at *Exhaust Fumes and French Fries*.

**Alistair Noon**'s chapbook, *At the Emptying of Dustbins*, recently appeared from Oystercatcher Press. He lives in Berlin.

**Claire Quigley** is a Glasgow-based photographer. She is interested in exploring the effects achievable using long-exposures, reflections, and alternative light-sources. She is the official photographer for the new Glasgow poetry society "Vital Synz."

**Steve Rago** is a publishing executive at John Wiley & Sons and is a former editor at *The New York Times*. His work has been shown in Manhattan and the New York suburbs.

**Monica Raymond**'s poetry has been included in numerous publications. Her play, *The Owl Girl*, won the Castillo Prize in political theatre.

**Jane Rice** lives in San Francisco and pursues her interests in poetry, art, and art history. Please visit Propolis Press for information about her letterpress chapbook entitled *Portrait Sitters*.

**William Sea** was born in Taipei, Taiwan and has lived most of his life in Texas and Mississippi. His poetry and fiction have appeared in several publications.

**Tom Sheehan** is the author of several novels whose works have appeared in numerous journals, magazines, and anthologies, including *Ocean Magazine* and *Perigee*.

**Don Skiles** is the author of *Miss America and Other Stories* (Marion Boyars), and *The James Dean Jacket Story* (Cross+Roads Press). He lives and works in San Francisco.

Prize-winning photographer **Anne Morrison Smyth** grew up in Ripton, Vermont and in Cambridge, Massachusetts. Anne's love for wildernesses of all kinds informs her work with an intimate, unflinching celebration of the diverse small realities that create a larger truth.

**Jessamyn Smyth** is a writer in all genres. Her work has been nominated for the Pushcart Prize and recognized in *Best American Short Stories 2006*; her plays have been produced by numerous theatres; her essays have aired on Public Radio; and her poetry and short prose have appeared in various electronic and print journals.

**Merry Speece** has published two chapbooks of poetry and been a recipient of a state arts commission fellowship in prose. Her *Sisters Grimke Book of Days* (Oasis Books, England) is a work of fragmented historical scholarship.

**Rick Spuler**'s writings have appeared in numerous literary magazines. Someday he'd like to write a book.

**Gregory Stapp** is a librarian by day and a writer by night, living and breathing in the middle-western wilds known as Oklahoma.

**Karen Stromberg** has recently turned to writing flash fiction and the 10-minute play. When not writing, she resuscitates books in the back room of a San Diego County Library.

**Elizabeth Kate Switaj** is the author of *Magdalene & the Mermaids* and two other books, and is the editor of *Crossing Rivers Into Twilight* and *Gender Across Borders*.

**Pia Taavila** is a Professor of English at Gallaudet University in Washington, DC. Her collection of poems, *Moon on the Meadow*, was published by the Gallaudet University Press in 2008.

**Eileen R. Tabios** is a prolific writer who received the Philippines' National Book Award for Poetry. She blogs as the "Chatelaine" and edits *Galatea Resurrects*, a popular poetry review journal.

**Ray Templeton** is a Scottish writer and musician living in St. Albans, England. His poetry and short fiction has appeared widely on the web as well as in print, and he is a member of the editorial board of *Blues & Rhythm* magazine.

**Judith Terzi** lives in Southern California where she taught high school French and college writing for many years. Her work has appeared or is forthcoming in numerous journals, most recently in *Eucalypt*, *Ginosko*, and *Red Rock Review*.

**Meredith Trede** writes, "When I'm paid with money for my work I'm a management consultant. Otherwise I'm a poet, parent, and publisher."

**Nico Vassilakis** is a multimedia artist, poet, and writer. His visual poetry videos have been shown worldwide at festivals and exhibitions of innovative language arts, and his writings have appeared in numerous magazines.

**Julene Tripp Weaver** works in HIV Services, and has a chapbook, *Case Walking: An AIDS Case Manager Wails Her Blues*, based on her work. A poem from this chapbook was featured on *The Writer's Almanac*.

**Holly Wehmeyer** grew up on a farm in northern Illinois and now writes poetry in Chicago. She has been published in *qarrtsiluni*'s "Journaling the Apocalypse" issue and in *righthandpointing* Issue #22, "Why Is It Starting Now?"

An Edinburgh-born poet and publisher with a scientific background, **Colin Will** now lives in Dunbar. He has always played an active part in developing Scotland's poetry organisations. His publishing house, Calder Wood Press, specialises in poetry chapbooks.

**Steve Wing** is a visual artist and writer whose work reflects his appreciation for the extraordinary in ordinary days and places. He lives in Florida, where he takes dawn photos on his way to work in an academic institution.

**Christopher Woods** is the author of a prose collection, *Under a Riverbed Sky*, and a collection of stage monologues for actors. His photography can be seen in his online gallery, Moonbird Hill Arts, which he shares with his wife.

**Rachel Woolf** says, "I prefer words and music or words and images to just words—just as food and company is so much more than just food. I am an advocate for the lullaby genre, which was the way I started writing and is still my first love."

**Gerard Wozek**'s first collection of poetry, *Dervish* (Gival Press, 2001) won the Gival Press Poetry Prize. He teaches literature and creative writing at Robert Morris University Illinois in Chicago and recently released a collection of short travel stories.